FOND DU LAC PUBLIC LIBRARY
WITHDRAWN

294.6

World Religions

SIKHISM

DiscoverRoo
An Imprint of Pop!
popbooksonline.com

by Elizabeth Andrews

WELCOME TO DiscoverRoo!

This book is filled with videos, puzzles, games, and more! Scan the QR codes* while you read, or visit the website below to make this book pop.

popbooksonline.com/sikhism

abdobooks.com

Published by Pop!, a division of ABDO, PO Box 398166, Minneapolis, Minnesota 55439. Copyright © 2024 by Abdo Consulting Group, Inc. International copyrights reserved in all countries. No part of this book may be reproduced in any form without written permission from the publisher. DiscoverRoo™ is a trademark and logo of Pop!.

Printed in the United States of America, North Mankato, Minnesota.
052023
082023

THIS BOOK CONTAINS RECYCLED MATERIALS

Cover Photo: Shutterstock Images
Interior Photos: Shutterstock Images, Getty Images, Wikimedia Commons, Design Pics Inc/Shutterstock

Editor: Tyler Gieseke
Series Designer: Laura Graphenteen

Library of Congress Control Number: 2022950563

Publisher's Cataloging-in-Publication Data
Names: Andrews, Elizabeth, author.
Title: Sikhism / by Elizabeth Andrews
Description: Minneapolis, Minnesota : Pop!, 2024 | Series: World religions | Includes online resources and index
Identifiers: ISBN 9781098244484 (lib. bdg.) | ISBN 9781098245184 (ebook)
Subjects: LCSH: Sikhism--Doctrines--Juvenile literature. | Spiritual life--Sikhism--Juvenile literature. | World religions--Juvenile literature. | Religious belief--Juvenile literature.
Classification: DDC 294.6--dc23

*Scanning QR codes requires a web-enabled smart device with a QR code reader app and a camera.

TABLE OF CONTENTS

CHAPTER 1
A New Faith 4

CHAPTER 2
The Ten Gurus 10

CHAPTER 3
The Life of Sikhs. 16

CHAPTER 4
Rituals and Holidays. 22

Making Connections. 30
Glossary 31
Index. 32
Online Resources 32

CHAPTER 1

A NEW FAITH

People follow different religions across the world. A religion is an organized practice of faith and **worship**. Sikhism is a new religion. It began only 500 years ago in Punjab, India.

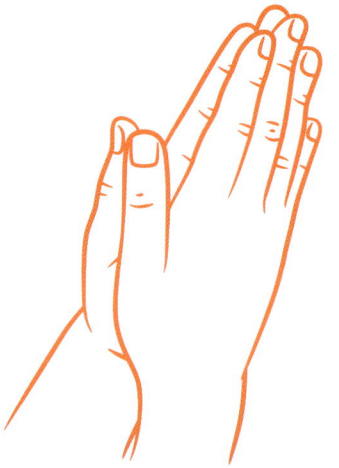

WATCH A VIDEO HERE!

SIKH SYMBOLS

Khanda — The middle sword is double edged. This connects the two other swords and reminds Sikhs that there is one God.

Chakkar — The circle in the middle represents God's **eternal** existence and love.

Miri — The sword on the left reminds Sikhs that they must fight for what is right in the world.

Piri — The sword on the right represents **spirituality**.

Sikhism is a religion that is full of color.

Sikhism is the fifth largest religion in the world with about 24 million followers. Most Sikhs, around 90 percent, live in India. The rest live around the world.

In 1499, a Hindu storekeeper named Nanak became the first Sikh guru. A guru is a religious master and teacher.

Nanak was taken up to the heavens by God. God gave him nectar to drink and told him, "Rejoice in my name and teach others to do so." God also told Nanak that all people are equal no matter their background. These points became the basis for Sikhism.

A man named Bhai Mardana (left) traveled with Nanak. He played music.

Guru Nanak returned to earth and his family. He quit his job and traveled for

Guru Nanak died in 1539.

20 years. He spoke about God and what he had seen. He gained followers who believed in the God Nanak met. Together, they formed the first community of Sikhs. They lived and worshipped God together.

During the next 500 years, Sikhism spread. The religion and its followers faced **opposition** from their Hindu and Muslim neighbors. Sikhs believe that all people are equal no matter what they believe. But other religions didn't like Sikhism and its growing popularity. Sikhs had to protect themselves and their homes.

CHAPTER 2
THE TEN GURUS

Guru Nanak was the first Sikh guru. Gurus guide Sikhs in their **worship** of God. There were ten human gurus from 1499 to 1708. Each guru named the next guru before their death. The gurus also wrote poems and religious songs called hymns.

LEARN MORE HERE!

Sikhs were forced to move around a lot. Gurus were in charge of picking new places to settle.

Sikh warriors fought battles and took home treasures.

Guru Nanak was followed by Guru Angad. He was wise and humble. Guru Angad helped Sikhism become an accepted religion in India. He also made the kitchens in gurdwaras free and available to all. A gurdwara is a Sikh house of worship.

The fourth was Guru Ram Das. He built the Sikh capital city of Amristar. It is home to the famous Golden Temple. The number of Sikhs had grown, so Ram Das began sending religious leaders called *masands* to **congregations**. Masands reported to the guru from each location.

DID YOU KNOW? The ninth guru, Guru Tegh Bahadur, was killed by the **Mughals** when they forced him to choose between joining Islam or death. This made him a **martyr**.

KHALSA

Khalsa means "pure." This religious order follows and protects Sikhism. Members go through a **ritual** to join the order. During the ritual they promise to follow strict rules. One of the rules is to not cut their hair.

All six of the following gurus were from the family of Guru Ram Das. The fifth guru, Guru Arjan, was the first to write down the hymns and poems of the earlier gurus. Guru Arjan and the Sikhs began to face **opposition** from Mughals. After that, Sikhs wore swords to protect themselves. Later gurus often led military battles as well as **spiritual** practices.

Guru Gobind Singh was the tenth and final human guru. He created a group of Sikh warriors called the Khalsa. Guru Gobind Singh chose the book of holy scriptures to be the next guru. The book contains all the hymns and teachings of the gurus.

Guru Gobind Singh was well educated. He knew many languages and wrote poetry.

CHAPTER 3
THE LIFE OF SIKHS

Guru Granth Sahib is the holy book of Sikhism. According to Sikhs, Guru Gobind Singh made the sacred text a living guru. It is made up of hymns from previous gurus. It also has stories about saints from Hinduism and Islam. Sikhs treat it with **devotion**, just as they treated the human gurus.

EXPLORE LINKS HERE!

Sikh men and women wear head coverings, such as scarves and turbans.

Turbans are wrapped in many different ways. The fabric is usually 18 feet (5.5m) long.

A Sikh is any person who believes in God, the teachings of the ten Gurus, and the Khalsa **ritual** called Amrit Sanskar.

The Sikh God is the same God other religions **worship**. Sikhs believe that God should always be on their mind. They read from Guru Granth Sahib and sing its hymns throughout the day.

Sikhs wake up early. They recite a morning hymn and listen to a broadcast from the Golden Temple. The broadcast serves as daily guidance for Sikhs. At the end of the day, they read scripture from Guru Granth Sahib. In all, Sikhs recite five prayers every day.

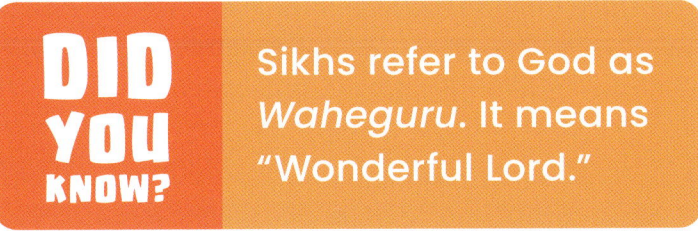

DID YOU KNOW?
Sikhs refer to God as *Waheguru.* It means "Wonderful Lord."

There is a Sikh code of conduct called the Sikh Rehat Maryada. It tells Sikhs how to follow the religion and live their lives the way God and the gurus want them to. This includes caring for the community, avoiding greed, **meditating**, and focusing on their bond with God.

Putting scripture to music is a way to communicate with God. Trained Sikh musicians who play at gurdwaras are called ragis.

CHAPTER 4
RITUALS AND HOLIDAYS

Guru Nanak did not want Sikhs to follow any rituals because he thought they were distractions from God. When the religion began, there were no **pilgrimages** or statues for **worship**. Pilgrimages to the Golden Temple became acceptable with

COMPLETE AN ACTIVITY HERE!

new gurus. There are still no statues. Sikhs believe they are meant to only worship God through Guru Granth Sahib.

The Golden Temple is the most important location in Sikhism. Sikhs have guarded it with their lives.

Sikhs fill the streets when it's time to celebrate Guru Granth Sahib.

Like most religions, Sikhism has holidays. A *gurpurb* is a celebration of the birth or death of a guru. Guru Nanak's birthday is the most important gurpurb. It lasts three days in November. The entire Guru Granth Sahib is read over 48 hours. Some people take a holy bath in the pond of the Golden Temple.

The Golden Temple sits in the middle of a pond called Amrita Saras, meaning "pool of nectar."

One of the most popular holidays is Baisakhi. It celebrates the first Khalsa warriors. People visit gurdwaras to

Gurdwaras have kitchens. The celebratory meals are made there.

A Khalsa warrior's sword is double edged. This means it is sharp on both sides.

read scripture and sing hymns as a community. There are special meals and treats. A parade is led by current warriors performing fighting demonstrations. Guru Granth Sahib ends the parade on a beautiful float.

During the Diwali holiday, many Sikhs visit the Golden Temple. They light oil lamps called diyas.

Children receive their names with a special Sikh tradition. Parents bring their babies to a gurdwara. There, an attendant opens Guru Granth Sahib at random. Parents pick a name with a first initial matching the first letter on the top left page of Guru Granth Sahib.

Sikhism is still not well known around the world. It is a religion that has long been fighting for its place. Through dedication and passion, the Sikh belief in freedom and love will continue to spread.

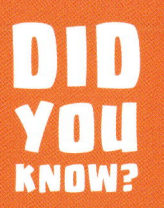

DID YOU KNOW? A Sikh name is followed by *Kaur*, meaning princess, for a girl or *Singh*, meaning lion, for a boy.

MAKING CONNECTIONS

TEXT-TO-SELF

What aspect of Sikhism most interested you? Please explain your answer.

TEXT-TO-TEXT

Have you read any books about different religions? How are those religions similar to or different from Sikhism?

TEXT-TO-WORLD

Sikhism is still not very well known to the world. How do you think the religion could spread around the world?

GLOSSARY

congregation — a religious community organized in a certain location.

devotion — strong affection, respect, and dedication.

eternal — lasting forever.

martyr — a person who willingly suffers death for refusing to leave a religion.

meditate — to practice quieting and transforming the mind.

Mughal — an Indian Muslim. Mughals ruled northern India between the 16th and 18th centuries.

opposition — one or more persons who are against someone or something.

pilgrimage — a journey taken to a shrine or holy place.

ritual — a set of actions always done in the same way.

spiritual — having to do with religious matters or people's beliefs in things such as the soul or what happens after death.

worship — love, respect, and affection shown to God.

INDEX

God, 5, 7, 9–10, 18–20, 22
Golden Temple, 13, 19, 22, 25
gurdwara, 12, 26, 29
Guru Angad, 12
Guru Arjan, 14
Guru Gobind Singh, 14, 16
Guru Granth Sahib, 16, 19, 23, 25, 27, 29
Guru Nanak, 6–10, 12, 22, 25
Guru Ram Das, 13–14

hymn, 10, 14–16, 19, 27
India, 4, 6, 12–13
Khalsa, 14, 18, 26
Mughals, 13–14
sword, 4, 14

This book is filled with videos, puzzles, games, and more! Scan the QR codes* while you read, or visit the website below to make this book pop.

popbooksonline.com/sikhism

*Scanning QR codes requires a web-enabled smart device with a QR code reader app and a camera.